BUILDING GENERATIONAL WEALTH

Proven tips and strategies for Long-term prosperity

Robert L. Calahan

TABLE OF CONTENTS

Chapter 1:Introduction

Generational wealth refers to assets passed down from one generation to another, providing financial security and opportunities for future descendants. Unlike short-term financial success, generational wealth focuses on creating a lasting legacy that benefits not only the current generation but also those to come. Understanding the concept of generational wealth is essential for individuals and families seeking to build a strong financial foundation that can withstand the test of time.

Why Building Generational Wealth Matters

Building generational wealth is about more than just accumulating money and assets. It's about creating a sense of security, stability, and opportunity for future generations. Here's why it matters:

1. **Financial Security**: Generational wealth provides a safety net for future generations, offering protection against unforeseen circumstances such as economic downturns, job loss, or medical emergencies. With a solid financial foundation in place, families can weather financial storms with greater resilience and confidence.

2. **Opportunity Creation**: By building generational wealth, families can create opportunities for their descendants to pursue their passions, interests, and goals without being constrained by financial limitations. Whether it's funding education, starting a business, or pursuing creative endeavors,

generational wealth opens doors to a world of possibilities.

3. **Breaking the Cycle of Poverty**: For many families, generational wealth represents a means of breaking the cycle of poverty and creating a brighter future for successive generations. By investing in education, homeownership, and entrepreneurship, families can empower their descendants to achieve economic independence and upward mobility.

4. **Legacy Building**: Building generational wealth allows families to leave a lasting legacy that extends beyond their own lifetimes. Whether through philanthropy, charitable giving, or passing down valuable assets and resources, families can make a positive impact on future generations and contribute to the greater good of society.

5. **Family Unity and Cohesion**: The process of building generational wealth often involves collaboration, communication, and shared values among family members. By working together towards common financial goals, families can strengthen bonds, foster unity, and instill a sense of purpose and identity that transcends individual wealth.

6. **Long-Term Financial Planning**: Generational wealth requires careful planning, foresight, and discipline. By adopting a long-term perspective on financial management, families can develop strategies for wealth preservation, growth, and transfer across multiple generations. This approach encourages financial responsibility, stewardship, and a commitment to the well-being of future descendants.

7. **Reducing Wealth Inequality**: In an era of growing wealth inequality, building generational wealth offers a means of leveling the playing field and promoting greater economic equity. By ensuring that wealth is passed down through generations, families can help bridge the gap between the haves and the have-nots and create a more just and equitable society.

Understanding generational wealth and actively working towards building it is essential for creating a secure, prosperous future for ourselves and future generations. By recognizing the importance of financial security, opportunity creation, legacy building, and family unity, we can lay the foundation for a brighter tomorrow and leave a lasting impact on the world. Building generational wealth is not just about accumulating riches; it's about investing in the future and shaping the destiny of generations to come.

Chapter 2: foundation of generational wealth

Building generational wealth starts with laying a strong foundation of financial education for future generations. In today's complex and ever-changing financial landscape, teaching young people about money management, investing, and wealth-building strategies is crucial for their long-term success. By providing them with the knowledge and skills they need to make informed financial decisions, we empower them to navigate the complexities of personal finance and build a solid financial future.

Why Financial Education Matters

1. **Empowerment**: Financial education empowers individuals to take control of their financial lives and make informed

decisions about money. By understanding basic financial concepts such as budgeting, saving, investing, and debt management, individuals can avoid common financial pitfalls and achieve their long-term financial goals.

2. **Building Wealth**: Knowledge is power when it comes to building wealth. By teaching young people about the power of compounding, the importance of investing early, and the various asset classes available, we equip them with the tools they need to grow their wealth over time. This sets them on the path towards financial independence and prosperity.

3. **Breaking the Cycle**: For many families, a lack of financial education perpetuates a cycle of poverty and financial insecurity across generations. By breaking this cycle and providing children with access to financial

education, we give them the opportunity to create a better future for themselves and their families. Financial education is the key to breaking down barriers and leveling the playing field for all individuals, regardless of their background or socioeconomic status.

4. **Fostering Responsible Citizenship**: In addition to personal financial benefits, financial education also fosters responsible citizenship and contributes to the overall well-being of society. Individuals who are financially literate are better equipped to make informed decisions about their finances, contribute to the economy, and participate actively in civic life. This strengthens communities and promotes social and economic stability.

Instilling a Wealth Mindset in Your Family

In addition to providing financial education, instilling a wealth mindset in your family is essential for building generational wealth. A wealth mindset goes beyond mere accumulation of money; it encompasses attitudes, beliefs, and behaviors that foster long-term financial success and abundance. By cultivating a wealth mindset within your family, you create a culture of prosperity, abundance, and possibility that transcends generations.

Key Principles of a Wealth Mindset

1. **Abundance Mentality**: A wealth mindset is rooted in the belief that there is more than enough abundance to go around. Instead of operating from a scarcity mentality, which focuses on limitations and lack, individuals with a wealth mindset embrace abundance and see opportunities everywhere.

2. **Financial Responsibility**: A wealth mindset emphasizes the importance of financial responsibility and stewardship. This means living within one's means, avoiding debt whenever possible, and making wise financial decisions that align with long-term goals.

3. **Embracing Risk**: Building wealth often requires taking calculated risks and stepping outside of one's comfort zone. Individuals with a wealth mindset are willing to embrace risk and see it as an opportunity for growth and expansion, rather than a threat to be avoided.

4. **Lifelong Learning**: A wealth mindset is characterized by a commitment to lifelong learning and personal growth. Individuals with a wealth mindset are constantly seeking new knowledge, skills, and opportunities for self-improvement, knowing that

continued growth is essential for long-term success.

5. **Gratitude and Generosity**: Finally, a wealth mindset is grounded in gratitude and generosity. Individuals with a wealth mindset appreciate the blessings in their lives and are eager to share their abundance with others. They understand that true wealth is not just about accumulating money, but about making a positive impact on the world and leaving a lasting legacy of generosity and kindness.

Building generational wealth requires laying a strong foundation of financial education and instilling a wealth mindset in your family. By providing young people with the knowledge, skills, and attitudes they need to succeed financially, we empower them to create a brighter future for themselves and future generations. Financial education and a wealth mindset are the cornerstones of generational wealth, setting the stage for long-term prosperity, abundance, and success.

Chapter 3: Building Blocks of Wealth

an era where financial stability transcends individual lifetimes, building generational wealth has become a cornerstone of financial planning. This essay delves into the foundational principles and practical strategies essential for securing long-term prosperity for future generations.

1. *Understanding the Building Blocks of Wealth:*

Generational wealth begins with a solid understanding of the fundamental building blocks of financial security. These include disciplined saving, strategic investing, and prudent risk management. By mastering these pillars, individuals can lay a robust foundation for wealth accumulation that spans generations.

2. *Investing Strategies for Long-Term Growth:*

A key component of generational wealth is the implementation of investment strategies geared towards long-term growth. This involves diversifying investment portfolios across various asset classes such as stocks, bonds, and real estate. Additionally, adopting a buy-and-hold approach and leveraging the power of compounding can exponentially grow wealth over time.

3. *Real Estate Investing and Property Ownership*:

Real estate stands out as one of the most reliable avenues for building generational wealth. Beyond providing a steady source of passive income through rental properties, real estate investments offer the potential for substantial appreciation over the years. Moreover, property ownership serves as a tangible asset that can be passed down to future generations, ensuring a lasting legacy of wealth.

4. *Entrepreneurship and Business Ownership*:

Entrepreneurship presents another avenue for creating generational wealth, offering the opportunity to build scalable businesses and create enduring value. By identifying market opportunities, fostering innovation, and cultivating resilience, entrepreneurs can generate substantial returns on investment that transcend their own lifetimes. Moreover, successful businesses can be passed down to successive generations, perpetuating a legacy of entrepreneurship and financial prosperity.

5. *Overcoming Challenges and Mitigating Risks*:

While the path to generational wealth is paved with opportunities, it is not without its challenges and risks. Economic downturns, market volatility, and unforeseen events can threaten financial stability if not adequately mitigated. Therefore, prudent risk management strategies, such as diversification, asset protection, and estate planning, are essential to safeguarding wealth across generations.

6. *Cultivating Financial Literacy and Education*:

Central to the preservation of generational wealth is the cultivation of financial literacy and education within families. By imparting sound financial principles, instilling disciplined saving habits, and fostering an entrepreneurial mindset, parents can empower their children to become stewards of wealth and continue the legacy of prosperity for future generations.

Building generational wealth is a multifaceted endeavor that requires a combination of foresight, discipline, and strategic planning. By embracing investment strategies such as real estate and entrepreneurship, individuals can create enduring legacies of prosperity that transcend their own lifetimes. Through prudent risk management, financial education, and a commitment to long-term growth, the pursuit of generational wealth becomes not only a personal aspiration but a testament to the enduring legacy of financial success.

Chapter 4: Preserving and Protecting Wealth

Building generational wealth begins with preserving and protecting what you have accumulated. This involves:

Long-Term Financial Planning: Establishing clear financial goals and implementing strategies to achieve them.

Diversification: Spreading ventures across various asset classes to diminish risk

Emergency Fund: Setting aside liquid assets to cover unexpected expenses and emergencies.

Insurance Coverage: Protecting against potential risks such as health issues, property damage, or liability claims.

Estate Planning: Ensuring the orderly transfer of assets to future generations while minimizing taxes and legal complications.

Estate Planning and Wealth Transfer Strategies

Estate planning plays a crucial role in passing down wealth to future generations. Key components include:

Wills and Trusts: Documenting your wishes regarding asset distribution and appointing guardians for minor children.

Asset Titling: Ensuring assets are titled properly to facilitate their transfer to heirs.

Beneficiary Designations: Specifying beneficiaries for retirement accounts, life insurance policies, and other assets.

Charitable Giving: Incorporating philanthropy into your estate plan to leave a legacy and potentially reduce estate taxes.

Regular Review and Updates: Periodically reviewing and updating your estate plan to reflect changes in your financial situation, family dynamics, and tax laws.

Tax Planning for Generational Wealth Preservation

Tax planning is essential for preserving generational wealth and maximizing its impact. Strategies may include:

Gift and Estate Taxes: Understanding tax thresholds and exemptions to minimize tax liabilities when transferring assets to heirs.

Gifting Strategies: Utilizing annual gift exclusions and lifetime gift exemptions to transfer assets tax-efficiently.

Trusts: Establishing trusts to hold and distribute assets according to your wishes while potentially reducing estate taxes.

Charitable Contributions: Leveraging charitable deductions to lower income and estate tax liabilities.

Roth Conversions: Converting traditional retirement accounts to Roth accounts to potentially reduce future tax burdens for heirs.

Asset Protection and Risk Management

Safeguarding assets from potential threats is essential for preserving generational wealth. This may involve:

Insurance Policies: Obtaining adequate insurance coverage for life, health, property, and liability risks.

Legal Structures: Establishing entities such as trusts, LLCs, or family limited partnerships to protect assets from creditors and legal claims.

Diversification: Spreading speculations across various resource classes and geographic areas to relieve market risk

Regular Monitoring and Adjustments: Continuously assessing risk exposure and adjusting asset protection strategies as needed to adapt to changing circumstances.

Building generational wealth is a multifaceted endeavor that requires careful planning and execution across various domains. By focusing on preserving and protecting wealth, implementing effective estate planning and wealth transfer strategies, engaging in proactive tax planning, and prioritizing asset protection and risk management, individuals can create a lasting legacy that benefits future generations for years to come.

Chapter 5: Navigating family dynamics

Building generational wealth through effective communication, collaboration, managing expectations, and creating a family legacy plan requires a comprehensive approach that addresses both financial and relational aspects.

Firstly, communication is key. Open and honest communication among family members is essential for understanding each other's goals, values, and concerns regarding wealth accumulation and distribution. Regular family meetings can provide a platform for discussing financial plans, investment strategies, and long-term goals. Additionally, fostering a culture of transparency can help mitigate misunderstandings and conflicts in the future.

Collaboration goes hand in hand with communication. By involving all family members in the decision-making process, you can harness the diverse skills, experiences, and perspectives within the family to develop robust wealth-building strategies. Encouraging active participation from younger generations not only instills a sense of ownership but also ensures continuity in managing family assets.

Managing expectations is crucial to maintaining harmony within the family. Setting realistic goals and boundaries around wealth can help prevent entitlement and promote gratitude and responsibility. Educating family members, especially younger ones, about the value of hard work, financial discipline, and the risks associated with wealth can instill a sense of appreciation and resilience.

Creating a family legacy plan involves defining and preserving the values, traditions, and assets that are important to the family across generations. This may include establishing trusts, wills, and other estate planning mechanisms to ensure a smooth transfer of wealth and minimize tax liabilities. Moreover, incorporating philanthropic initiatives into the legacy plan can not only leave a positive impact on society but also foster a sense of unity and purpose among family members.

In summary, building generational wealth requires more than just financial acumen—it requires effective communication, collaboration, managing expectations, and creating a shared vision for the future. By prioritizing these aspects and integrating them into a comprehensive family legacy plan, you can lay the foundation for prosperity that extends beyond individual lifetimes.

Chapter 6: Philanthropy and Social Responsibility

Philanthropy and social responsibility are integral aspects of corporate and individual values, emphasizing the importance of giving back to the community and making a positive impact on society. Philanthropy goes beyond monetary donations; it encompasses volunteerism, advocacy, and corporate social responsibility initiatives aimed at addressing social, environmental, and economic challenges.

Giving Back to the Community:

Giving back to the community involves actively contributing resources, time, and expertise to support local or global causes. This can take various forms, including charitable donations to nonprofits, volunteering at community organizations, and initiating social impact projects. Through giving back, individuals and organizations can address pressing issues such as poverty, education inequality, healthcare access, and environmental conservation.

Incorporating Social Impact into Wealth Management:

Wealth management traditionally focused solely on financial returns, but there's a growing recognition of the importance of incorporating social impact into investment strategies. Impact investing, sustainable investing, and Environmental, Social, and Governance (ESG) criteria are gaining traction among investors who seek to generate positive societal and environmental outcomes alongside financial returns. Wealth managers now have the opportunity to align their clients' investment goals with their values, contributing to meaningful change while building wealth.

Building Generational Wealth:

Building generational wealth involves creating and preserving assets that can be passed down to future generations. While financial wealth is important, generational wealth also encompasses intangible assets such as education, values, and social capital. Incorporating social impact into wealth management strategies can help families leave a legacy that goes beyond monetary inheritance, instilling values of social responsibility, empathy, and stewardship in the next generation. By investing in companies and initiatives that prioritize environmental sustainability, social equity, and ethical business practices, families can build a legacy of positive impact that extends far beyond their lifetimes.

Case Studies and Examples:

Numerous examples illustrate the intersection of philanthropy, social responsibility, and wealth management. Families like the Gates, Buffet, and Rockefeller have established foundations and initiatives dedicated to addressing global challenges such as healthcare, education, and poverty. Companies like Patagonia, Unilever, and Tesla have integrated sustainability into their business models, demonstrating that social responsibility can be profitable and contribute to long-term success.

Challenges and Opportunities:

Despite the growing momentum behind socially responsible investing, there are challenges to overcome. Measurement and evaluation of social impact can be complex, requiring standardized metrics and transparent reporting. Additionally, there may be perceived trade-offs between financial returns and social impact, although evidence suggests that companies with strong ESG practices can outperform their peers over the long term. Wealth managers must navigate these challenges while seizing the opportunities presented by the shift towards sustainable and impact investing.

philanthropy, social responsibility, and wealth management are interconnected disciplines that play a crucial role in building generational wealth. By giving back to the community, incorporating social impact into investment strategies, and embracing values of stewardship and sustainability, individuals and families can leave a lasting legacy that enriches both society and future generations. As the world faces increasingly complex challenges, the integration of social impact into wealth management is not only a moral imperative but also a strategic opportunity to create positive change while building wealth.

Chapter 7: Adapting to Changing Times

To build generational wealth, adapting to changing times is crucial. This entails staying ahead of economic and technological trends, fostering flexibility, and fostering innovation in wealth-building strategies. Adapting to these changes ensures that wealth is not only created but also preserved and multiplied for future generations.

Economic and technological landscapes are constantly evolving, presenting both challenges and opportunities for wealth building. Keeping abreast of these changes allows individuals and families to anticipate shifts in markets, industries, and consumer behavior, enabling them to adjust their wealth-building approaches accordingly.

Technological advancements, in particular, have revolutionized the way wealth is generated and managed. From the rise of fintech platforms to the growing influence of artificial intelligence in investment strategies, embracing innovation is key to staying competitive in today's fast-paced world.

Flexibility is another essential component of successful wealth building. Markets can be unpredictable, and rigid strategies may not always yield the desired results. By maintaining a flexible mindset, individuals can pivot when necessary, seizing new opportunities and mitigating risks along the way.

Moreover, innovation plays a vital role in wealth accumulation. Whether it's identifying untapped markets, developing groundbreaking products, or implementing cutting-edge financial tools, innovative thinking sets the stage for long-term prosperity.

One strategy for building generational wealth is investing in assets that appreciate over time, such as real estate, stocks, and businesses. However, the key is not just to accumulate assets but to manage them wisely. This involves diversifying investments to spread risk, conducting thorough research before making investment decisions, and regularly reviewing and adjusting portfolios to adapt to changing market conditions.

Another approach is to focus on income generation through entrepreneurial endeavors or passive income streams. Creating multiple streams of income provides a more stable financial foundation and increases the likelihood of long-term wealth accumulation.

In addition to traditional wealth-building methods, it's essential to explore alternative avenues for growth. This could include investing in emerging industries like renewable energy or blockchain technology, or leveraging opportunities in global markets through international diversification.

Furthermore, embracing sustainable practices can contribute to both financial success and a positive impact on future generations. Investing in environmentally friendly businesses or supporting socially responsible initiatives not only aligns with ethical values but can also generate attractive returns over the long term.

Education and mentorship are also invaluable tools in building generational wealth. By continuously learning from experts and seeking guidance from experienced individuals, one can acquire the knowledge and skills needed to navigate complex financial landscapes and make informed decisions.

Effective estate planning is essential for preserving wealth and ensuring a smooth transfer of assets to future generations. This involves creating wills, trusts, and other legal structures to protect assets from taxes, creditors, and other potential threats, while also providing for the financial well-being of heirs and beneficiaries.

Building generational wealth requires a proactive approach that prioritizes adaptation, flexibility, and innovation. By staying ahead of economic and technological trends, embracing flexibility in wealth-building strategies, and fostering innovation in investment approaches, individuals and families can create a legacy of prosperity that lasts for generations to come.

Chapter 8 :Conclusion

In conclusion, the pursuit of generational wealth is not merely about accumulating riches for oneself, but about establishing a lasting legacy that can benefit future generations. Throughout this book, we have delved into various key strategies that can aid in the creation and preservation of generational wealth. From prudent financial planning to savvy investment decisions, each step plays a crucial role in laying the foundation for long-term prosperity.

One of the fundamental pillars of building generational wealth is a commitment to long-term financial success. This entails cultivating disciplined saving habits, living within one's means, and making strategic investments that have the potential to grow over time. By prioritizing long-term goals over short-term gratification, individuals can harness the power of compounding interest and asset appreciation to steadily increase their wealth over the years.

Moreover, a diversified investment portfolio is essential for mitigating risk and maximizing returns. By spreading investments across different asset classes such as stocks, bonds, real estate, and alternative investments, individuals can reduce their exposure to market volatility and enhance the overall resilience of their wealth-building strategy. Additionally, periodic rebalancing of the portfolio ensures that it remains aligned with changing market conditions and investment objectives.

Furthermore, fostering a culture of financial education within the family is paramount for ensuring the sustainability of generational wealth. By imparting valuable knowledge about budgeting, saving, investing, and estate planning to future generations, families can empower their heirs to make informed financial decisions and carry forward the legacy of wealth stewardship. Inculcating values of prudence, frugality, and resilience can help instill a sense of responsibility and accountability in heirs, ensuring that the wealth accumulated over generations is preserved and utilized judiciously.

In addition to prudent financial management, proactive estate planning is crucial for protecting and transferring generational wealth to subsequent generations. Establishing trusts, wills, and other legal structures can help minimize estate taxes, avoid probate, and ensure that assets are distributed according to the wishes of the benefactor. Moreover, regular reviews and updates to the estate plan are necessary to accommodate changes in family dynamics, tax laws, and financial circumstances.

Beyond financial considerations, building generational wealth also entails fostering strong family relationships and instilling a sense of shared purpose and responsibility among family members. Open communication, trust, and mutual respect form the bedrock of successful multigenerational wealth management. By involving family members in financial discussions and decision-making processes, individuals can promote unity, cohesion, and a shared commitment to the long-term prosperity of the family legacy.

In conclusion, the pursuit of generational wealth requires a multifaceted approach that encompasses prudent financial management, proactive estate planning, and the cultivation of strong family values. By adhering to the key strategies outlined in this book and maintaining a steadfast commitment to long-term financial success, individuals can create a lasting legacy that transcends generations and empowers their descendants to thrive economically, socially, and culturally. Ultimately, building generational wealth is not just about amassing riches; it is about investing in the future and leaving behind a legacy of opportunity, security, and prosperity for generations to come.